RATIONAL DRINKING

HOW TO LIVE HAPPILY WITH OR WITHOUT ALCOHOL

MICHAEL R. EDELSTEIN, PH.D.

with
WILL ROSS

Cover design by *GoOnWrite*

CONTENTS

1. YES, YOU CAN CONTROL YOUR DRINKING 5

2. THE UPSIDE OF DRINKING 9

3. DO YOU HAVE A DRINKING PROBLEM?................. 12

4. NINE GOOD REASONS TO CONTROL YOUR DRINKING 15

5. SIX STEPS FOR INCREASING YOUR WILLPOWER. 19

6. A LITTLE-KNOWN FACT ABOUT EXCESSIVE DRINKING 23

7. LONG-TERM VERSUS SHORT-TERM HAPPINESS .. 26

8. FIVE CRAZY SIGNS OF DRINKING THINKING 29

9. SEVEN QUESTIONS TO DRIVE YOU SANE 33

10. THE ABC'S OF EXCESSIVE DRINKING..................... 39

11. HOW TO CONTROL YOUR DRINKING IN THREE MINUTES... 43

12. DO YOU REALLY NEED A DRINK?........................... 47

13. SOBRIETY IS NOT THE END OF THE WORLD 50

14. HOW TO COPE WITH BEING SOBER 54

15. HOW SELF-ABUSE LEADS TO ALCOHOL ABUSE 58

16. WILL SOBRIETY MAKE YOU A BETTER PERSON?61

17. HOW TO STOP BEATING YOURSELF UP................ 65

18. WHAT'S LOVE GOT TO DO WITH IT? 69

19. PERFECTIONISM, BOOZE AND YOU 76

20. DO OTHER PEOPLE DRIVE YOU TO DRINK? 83

21. HOW TO THINK YOUR WAY TO SOBRIETY 90

22. HOW TO CHANGE THE WAY YOU FEEL ABOUT ALCOHOL 96

23. ACTIONS SPEAK LOUDER THAN WORDS 100

24. GETTING ON WITH GETTING SOBER 103

CONTACT DR. EDELSTEIN 106

ABOUT THE AUTHORS 108

1. YES, YOU CAN CONTROL YOUR DRINKING

IF YOU'VE MADE THE DECISION TO REDUCE your alcohol consumption or to quit drinking altogether – or if you're only thinking about it – this book is for you.

If you're tired of spending your hard-earned cash on booze, if you're tired of always being hung over, if you're tired of damaging your health and relationships because you drink so much, then this book speaks to you.

Perhaps you've attempted to quit many times without success. Perhaps you've tried Alcoholics Anonymous or other self-help programs, only to find they didn't work.

Whether you're quitting for the first time, or you've quit many times only to return to drink, you're ready to abandon ineffective methods that don't get at the core of your problem.

Now there's a proven way to take charge of your drinking and your life.

This practical, effective way is called Rational Emotive Behavior Therapy (REBT) and was devised by the pioneering psychologist, Dr. Albert Ellis. Our book describes how to use REBT to master your drinking. The good news is you're not powerless!

To control your drinking, use the REBT concepts and strategies conscientiously and you're sure to succeed. If your goal consists of abstinence, you can accomplish this by diligently employing the approach we'll teach you. If you wish to drink moderately, these recommendations are applicable as well.

Our book won't tell you to stop drinking. It won't tell you to reduce the amount you drink. It won't tell you to drink less often. You don't need a book to tell you this. You can make these decisions yourself based on your unique values and circumstances. It's your life and it's up to you to choose your objectives.

But once you've chosen your goal, we'll teach you powerful concepts and strategies to achieve it.

How do you decide if your drinking presents a problem? If your drinking blocks, sabotages, or interferes with your long-term goals, then it's a problem. Consequently, if you've determined it's best to drink no more than one glass of wine per day and you succeed, then by this criteria you don't have a problem. But if your goal is to drink no wine at all, and you drink a glass – or more – a day, then you do have a problem.

Whether you have a problem is not based on how much you drink, *per se*; it's based on how well your drinking habits conform to your goals. If you believe your drinking pattern is counterproductive, this is a problem. Always start and end with your goals and objectives in mind.

As a consequence of my long experience helping compulsive drinkers, I've observed over and over the patterns that do work and those that don't work. We'll explain why, despite your best intentions, you find it so difficult to drink reasonably.

You can begin using REBT's powerful tools today to take control of your drinking and your life.

2. THE UPSIDE OF DRINKING

PEOPLE DRINK ALCOHOL FOR THREE major reasons: to escape discomfort, to enhance good feelings, and to improve behavior.

Imbibing to escape discomfort includes drowning your sorrows, coping with loneliness, boredom, the stresses of a difficult job, and depression. Also, as a procrastination strategy, to avoid facing hassles such as dealing with your poor finances or your crumbling marriage.

Drinking to enhance positive feelings may involve celebrating a win or the completion of a difficult task, relaxing with friends, having a good time at a party, reliving fond memories, enjoying the taste of the drink or the taste of a good meal. Some medical authorities also suggest there are health benefits with moderate usage.

Drinking to improve behavior includes getting your creative juices flowing, falling asleep, doing better at a job interview, or interacting more easily at a party. (We're not saying any of these attempts are effective, only that some people believe they will be!)

People who drink alcohol for these reasons all have one thing in common: they all wish to improve their lives, by feeling or doing better (at least for the moment) than they would have had they abstained.

A major problem with all this involves the inevitability that, if they drink beyond a certain point, sooner or later the good feelings will be replaced by bad feelings. In other words, moderate alcohol consumption helps most individuals feel better; excessive alcohol consumption makes them feel worse.

Life is often difficult and filled with hassles. With all the drudgery and turmoil life throws at us, it makes sense to desire to feel better. It's human nature to do what we can to rid ourselves of bad feelings, and do what we can to make ourselves feel good and perform well. After all, since we have only one life, why not enjoy it as much as we possibly can? And if moderate alcohol consumption can help us enjoy some moments, then why not drink?

Most people can get the benefits of alcohol without overindulging, without drinking so much they no longer feel good. Sadly for many others, drinking alcohol is a problem; once they start drinking they continue way beyond the point of feeling good. They drink so much and so often they put their health, jobs, and relationships in jeopardy.

Whether you drink in moderation or excess, you drink for one reason: at the moment you decide to drink you've convinced yourself the alcohol will improve your life.

3. DO YOU HAVE A DRINKING PROBLEM?

YOU MAY BE WONDERING IF YOU HAVE a drinking problem. Perhaps you're concerned about the amount you drink and the frequency with which you drink. Or maybe your friends or family members have commented about your drinking. You may be wondering, "Am I addicted to alcohol? Am I an alcoholic?" When it comes to drinking, it all boils down to one question: what are my goals?

Mary loves her husband, adores her two young kids, and loves to get drunk. Her favorite drink is vodka because, she says, it gets her drunk quicker than any other alcoholic beverage. She drinks every night, either socially or alone. She enjoys being drunk and is not the least concerned with the long-term health risks. She would rather live a short, drunk, and merry life than a long, sober, and healthy life. Although some of her friends and family are worried about her drinking habits, Mary is happy to go on as she is.

William, her older single brother, is different from Mary. He, too, likes to drink but is concerned about the amount he drinks. He doesn't drink as much as Mary nor as often, but he would still like to cut down. He's tried reducing the amount he drinks, and has occasionally abstained for weeks at a time. When he goes out, William would like to restrict himself to just one or two drinks but invariably ends up drinking considerably more. He's tried to quit several times but has found it challenging. He continues to drink despite his best intentions.

You'll notice William and Mary have different drinking objectives. Mary's goal is to drink a lot and drink often. William's goal involves at least reducing his intake or perhaps quitting altogether.

Do both William and Mary have a problem?

The answer lies not in the amount they drink but in their goals. Even though Mary drinks more than William, she doesn't have a drinking problem. Her goal is to get drunk and she's achieving this goal. William, on the other hand, does have a problem. He wants to reduce or quit yet he continues to drink – sometimes excessively. He's failing at his goal.

To determine if you have a drinking problem, first decide on a goal. Would you be happy continuing as you are, without changing the quantity or the frequency of your drinking? If the answer is yes you're happy with your present habits, considering both your immediate and long-term goals, then you don't have a problem.

On the other hand, if you wish to reduce or quit but find you continually fail, then you do have a problem. Read on to learn how to overcome your problem and reach your goal by moderating the amount you drink or by quitting altogether.

4. NINE GOOD REASONS TO CONTROL YOUR DRINKING

PERHAPS YOU'D LIKE TO REDUCE THE amount of alcohol you drink. Or maybe you wish to drink less frequently. You may even want to quit drinking forever. You could have made this decision for a number of reasons including one or more of the following:

1. You're broke. You're fed up with spending your hard-earned money on booze. You have little or nothing in savings and struggle to pay your bills each month because you spend so much on alcohol. Perhaps you've even lost your home because you hadn't paid your mortgage or your rent.

2. Your health is deteriorating. After years of heavy drinking, you're noticing the effects on your health. Perhaps your doctor has confirmed your worst fears and informed you that you have a serious medical problem such as gastritis, cirrhosis, hepatitis, or pancreatitis.

3. You're overweight or obese. The high caloric content of alcohol is showing itself around your middle and elsewhere. The clothes you wore last year don't fit you anymore. You're constantly updating your wardrobe as your size continues to grow.

4. Your relationships are falling apart. Your friends and family have deserted you or are threatening to desert you. You can no longer count on the people you used to, and they certainly can't count on you.

5. You're unemployed. Turning up at work drunk or with a hangover – or not turning up at all – has led to losing your job. Again!

6. Your sex life is destructive. You're sleeping with strangers and engaging in risky sex you would avoid if you were sober. If you're male, you may have Brewer's droop and find your erections are not as strong as you'd like.

7. You risk DUIs. You may have even lost your driver's license. Worse, you could be facing a jail term – or a second one.

8. You provoke fights. When you drink you become aggressive and pick fights with friends or strangers.

9. You believe enough is enough. You're sick of all the trouble drinking has got you into, the harm it has done to your health and friendships, and you hate feeling ashamed, guilty, and embarrassed about your drinking.

Let's face it: there are innumerable convincing reasons to stop drinking. Perhaps none of the above problems apply to you but you fear they soon will. Or maybe you have other reasons not listed. No matter what your particular incentives, you've made the decision to quit. The next step involves turning your decision into action. We'll help you convert your good intentions into life-enhancing results.

5. SIX STEPS FOR INCREASING YOUR WILLPOWER

MANY INDIVIDUALS WHO FAIL TO QUIT drinking claim they lack willpower. This raises an important question: what *is* willpower?

Willpower is an ability we all have. The issue is whether we use it destructively or constructively. If you have a problem this means you've willfully developed, then stubbornly practiced, your drinking habit. Despite all the difficulties and red flags urging you to desist you doggedly keep at it. This takes commitment, determination, and willpower!

Once you've established the goal to stop or moderate your drinking, redirect the will you've been using destructively into constructive thinking and acting. This involves a series of steps. Let's examine each of the six steps.

1. Decide on your objective. Is it to quit now for good? Or is it to moderate? If the latter, specify in detail what your moderation will consist of, e.g., no drinking alone and no more than one drink on weekend evenings socially.

2. Decide when you will make this change. This step is a recognition of your desire and your ability to succeed. On its own, it's not enough. Wishing to stop and setting a date does not mean you'll act on it. The next four steps will turn your desire into action.

3. Make yourself determined to change your drinking habits. Resolve that *no matter what* you'll do whatever it takes to achieve your goal, no excuses and no debates!

4. Learn what you can about alcohol addiction and how to overcome it. Seek out cognitive, emotive, and behavioral ways to reach your goal. (Reading the rest of this book will be a great start!) Then practice, practice, practice.

5. Take action. Drink only as much as you plan to and no more. If you've decided to quit altogether, then stop drinking now.

6. Have a plan to deal with backsliding. It's not easy to change, and you may often take missteps and return to your old ways. But you're prepared because you recognize that, like everyone else on the planet, you're a fallible human being who often makes mistakes. You know that learning frequently involves two steps forward and one step back. You don't let that deter you. You're determined to succeed, so instead of abandoning your goal when you lapse, you make yourself even more resolved not to give up.

Using your willpower constructively means changing your thinking and taking action; it means working hard to reinforce new habits and refusing to give in to failure. You may dream of easy ways to control your alcohol consumption, but they don't exist. Unfortunately, in life there's seldom meaningful gain without pain.

6. A LITTLE-KNOWN FACT ABOUT EXCESSIVE DRINKING

A S WE'VE ALREADY SEEN, PEOPLE – including you – mainly drink alcohol to feel better. Yet why is it that while others limit their drinking, you feel unable to?

We've also seen it's human nature to want to avoid unpleasant feelings and have good feelings. People who drink too much go one step further: they *insist* – they *demand* – that they *must* avoid unpleasant feelings and only have good feelings.

The reason you drink more, or more often, than you want is you believe you *must* feel better or escape discomfort. You've escalated your strong *desire* to feel good into a *demand* to feel good and escape discomfort. This *thinking* causes you to drink excessively.

Having convinced yourself you must feel better and drink alcohol, you further convince yourself you *can't stand* to deprive yourself and *must* have another drink. You've convinced yourself it will be *terrible*, *awful*, and the *end of the world* if you don't have another drink.

There is one cause – and only one cause – of excessive drinking: the demand that you *must* avoid discomfort and you *have to* get the good feelings that come from drinking. You become addicted to alcohol when you tell yourself you *can't stand* discomfort and *gotta* avoid it – and the best way to avoid discomfort is to get drunk. Because you convince yourself you *must* avoid discomfort and get drunk you feel compelled to drink. In effect, you've given yourself no choice – you *must* drink; you're convinced you *absolutely need* a drink. With these beliefs you've effectively addicted yourself to the bottle.

The cause of being addicted to alcohol has little, if anything, to do with your childhood, your dysfunctional family, your job, your relationships, your financial status, or anything that has ever happened to you. And you do not have a disease!

It's your beliefs – specifically the belief that you *need* to escape bad feelings and have good feelings – that cause you to drink excessively. It's the belief that you *must* feel happy and *must not* feel unhappy that causes you to take another gulp.

If you passionately *desired* to feel better, without demanding you *must*, and you convinced yourself you never *need* another drink, you'd be in control of your drinking habits.

7. LONG-TERM VERSUS SHORT-TERM HAPPINESS

MOST PEOPLE WANT TO BE HAPPY. WE want to be happy when we're by ourselves, when we're with others – especially when we're with our significant other – when we're at work or school, and during our leisure time.

We're quite resourceful in finding ways to make ourselves happy. We can do it in simple ways such as by listening to music, watching a movie or play, or going to a sporting event. Or we can do it in more creative ways such as by building a yacht and sailing around the world, writing a book, getting a postgraduate degree, or training to run a marathon.

Some forms of happiness can be acquired quite quickly and easily while others take time and effort. Both ways of seeking happiness are legitimate and each has its place in our lives.

But sometimes in our quest to find short-term – quick and easy – happiness we sabotage our goal of long-term happiness. For example, if you spend all your disposable income going to concerts and movies, this may mean forfeiting your goal to see the world since you've no money left over for travel.

Similarly, if you drink frequently and copiously in a quest to find short-term happiness, you may damage your health and risk losing any chance of leading a long and healthy life.

You risk your long-term happiness when you insist – *demand* – that you *must* be happy right now, even if that means missing out on what you want in the long run.

Here's how it works. You begin with a *desire* to get rid of bad feelings and replace them with good feelings. Then you escalate your desire for good feelings into a *demand* for the good feelings you get from imbibing by convincing yourself you absolutely *need* a drink. Do this often enough and sooner or later your short-term indulgence destroys any hope you have for long-term happiness.

If you're like most people, you have a goal to lead a long, healthy, happy life. This may be the most important goal you'll ever have. But by drinking too much, too often, you replace what you *desire* most with what you tell yourself you *must* have right now. In other words it's your view, your belief, in the *need* for short-term escape that ultimately destroys your chances of long-term happiness. Compulsively going for short-term happiness sabotages deep satisfaction and fulfillment in life.

8. FIVE CRAZY SIGNS OF DRINKING THINKING

W E HUMAN BEINGS OFTEN ACT QUITE sanely. This keeps us alive. If we weren't reasonable, we wouldn't have the good sense to earn our bread when we're hungry, pay bills when they're due, and find relationships when we're lonely.

As realistic as we are, we can also act quite crazily, often behaving in ways that interfere with our short- and long-term health and happiness. For example, we get angry at our car or computer when they don't run smoothly despite the fact that machines have no way of detecting or responding to our rage. We put off going to see the doctor or dentist even though it's in our best interest to see them as scheduled. And, of course, we often drink alcohol more frequently and more copiously than is good for us.

More often than not, our self-defeating behavior is caused by ignorance or irrational beliefs. Irrational beliefs usually have one or more of the following characteristics:

1. Although they seem true and sensible to us at the time, upon closer examination, it's quite easy to see they're false and nonsensical.

2. They often lead to us thinking less of ourselves and putting ourselves down as unworthy human beings.

3. They interfere with our relationships making it difficult for us to get along with others.

4. They make us sedentary and unproductive.

5. They prevent us from reaching our short-term and –
more frequently – our long-term goals.

So where do these irrational beliefs come from?

For the most part, we're *born* with the tendency to
overgeneralize, condemn, and absolutize. These irrational
proclivities appear across all cultures and throughout all
of history. None of us is immune to them. Even
psychologists – who you might think would know better
– are prone to them.

Further evidence we're born with this unreasonable
proclivity comes from the observation that despite our
best efforts to act reasonably, unaffected by irrational
thinking, we often continue to resort to self-defeating
behavior. Additionally, we continue to act in self-
defeating ways even though our actions are frowned upon
by our friends and family, and even when we dislike our
own behavior.

As well as being born with a tendency to subscribe to
irrational beliefs, our culture, media, parents, teachers,
and our friends often reinforce our irrational beliefs. They
sometimes tell us such nonsense as, "You *must* do this

and you *must not* do that, and if you do otherwise you're a failure."

But by far the greatest influence on clinging to our irrational beliefs is our own self-talk. We constantly reinforce our irrational beliefs telling ourselves the same old nonsense over and over: "I *must* have a drink; I *need* a drink right now; I *must* get the good feelings that come from alcohol, and I *must* get them right now, else life is *terrible* and *I can't stand it*."

9. SEVEN QUESTIONS TO DRIVE YOU SANE

AS WE'VE ALREADY SEEN, YOUR STRUGGLE to quit or cut down your alcohol intake is sabotaged by irrational beliefs standing between you and your goals. These beliefs include the idea that you *have to* get rid of bad feelings and replace them with the good feelings you get from alcohol, otherwise you *can't stand it*.

A constructive battle with the bottle begins with a war on these destructive beliefs. The strategy for destroying these beliefs involves these four steps:

1. Identify the irrational beliefs that interfere, such as "I absolutely *must* satisfy my urge to drink, right now!"

2. Once you've identified these beliefs, question and challenge them. This means searching for supporting evidence for these notions. Ask yourself, "What is the evidence I absolutely *must* (rather than strongly prefer to) satisfy my urge?"

3. Prove to yourself your thinking is false, nonsensical, and destructive. In particular, convince yourself it's not a *necessity* to rid yourself of bad feelings and have only good feelings. Show yourself this belief makes no sense and is destructive. Reinforce the notion there are no *musts*, *shoulds*, *have tos*, or dire *necessities*. You don't run the universe so nothing *has to* be your way. You don't have perfect control over your body, mind, feelings, or circumstances, so an ideal state is never in the cards, although it would be lovely if it were.

4. As you uproot your addictive thinking, also reinforce constructive beliefs that are realistic, logical, and pragmatic i.e., they aid you in achieving better self-control. Practice telling yourself you *can survive* quite well if you

don't give in to the pleasure of the moment. Further, convince yourself that you *can bear* facing discomfort – even great discomfort – without the bottle.

Proving to yourself the beliefs leading to excessive drinking are false is the most important step. It is the *vital key* to controlling your drinking. You can show yourself your goal-sabotaging beliefs are false, illogical, and destructive by challenging them with these key questions:

1. Is this idea consistent with the facts? Is it true?

2. What evidence is there of the falseness of this belief?

3. Does this idea follow consistently from my values and preferences? Is it logical?

4. Does this idea help me reach my long-term goals? Is it pragmatic?

5. What are better, alternative ideas which are realistic, logical, and pragmatic?

6. What is the worst that's likely to happen if I don't get what I think I *must*?

7. What are some positive things that could happen – or I could make happen – if I don't get what I think I absolutely *must*?

Let's apply these seven key questions to one of the beliefs we've identified as standing in the way of reaching your long-term health goals. Let's examine the belief, "I *must* get rid of bad feelings and replace them with the good feelings I get from alcohol."

1. *Is it true? Is this idea consistent with the facts?* This idea is inconsistent with the facts. There is nothing in reality to support the idea that I *must* ever get rid of bad feelings, including urges, cravings, stress, or depression. There never exists any evidence, data, or proof for these psychopathological absolutes.

2. *What evidence is there for the falseness of this belief?* I've survived these uncomfortable feelings without alcohol many times in the past. The bad feelings have always waxed and waned.

3. *Is it logical? Does this idea follow consistently from my values and preferences?* It does not follow logically that because I

would *like* to be rid of them, therefore I *must* be rid of them. A preference can't magically turn into a necessity. Making my strong *desire* into a demand is a non-sequitur. Therefore, the idea that I *must* replace my bad feelings with good feelings fails a logical analysis.

4. *Is it pragmatic? Does this idea help me reach my long-term goals?* Clearly it does not help me reach my long-term goals because whenever I have this thought and act on it I violate my drinking goals. The idea that I *must* replace my bad feelings with the good feelings does not work for me.

5. *What are realistic, logical, and pragmatic perspectives I can reinforce instead?* Since the idea that I *must* get rid of my bad feelings and replace them with the good feelings is false, illogical, and unhelpful, its negation is true, logical, and helpful. Therefore a better, alternative would be, "I definitely *do not have to* replace my bad feelings with the good feelings I get from alcohol!" Also, "I *can stand* bad feelings, even though I distinctly dislike them."

6. *What is the worst that is likely to happen if I don't get what I think I must?* The likely worst case scenario if I don't drown my bad feelings in drink is that I'll feel bad for awhile! I may not enjoy the party as much or fit in as well

with my drinking buddies. But as we saw earlier, "No pain, no gain!"

7. *What are some positive things that could happen – or I could make happen – if I don't get what I think I must?* I could beat my alcohol addiction, eliminate uncomfortable cravings, feel healthier, improve my relationships, and increase my work productivity.

Practicing these seven key questions and answers will result in a more rational attitude toward alcohol. This will help you cut down or quit your alcohol consumption and help you reach your long-term health goals.

10. THE ABC'S OF EXCESSIVE DRINKING

THE IDEAS IN THIS BOOK ARE BASED ON the teachings of Dr Albert Ellis who, in 1955, created what was then a brand-new type of psychotherapy which is now called Rational Emotive Behavior Therapy (REBT). REBT was the first cognitive behavior therapy and has proven to be effective in treating a large number of emotional and behavioral problems – including alcohol dependence and abuse.

Albert Ellis developed a simple ABC model which he used to teach his clients how to be their own therapist. In this model, **A** stands for the Activating Event – the situation you were in or the feeling you had before you started drinking; **B** stands for your unhelpful Beliefs about the activating event; and **C** stands for the Consequences of combining A with B. Here's how it looks:

A. (Activating event): Something happens or you have a particular thought or feeling.

B. (irrational Belief): You have a demand – a *must*, *should*, or *have to* – about the situation.

C. (Consequences): You react to the situation in an unhelpful way.

When it comes to sabotaging your long-term health goals by drinking excessively, the ABC model looks like this:

A. (Activating event): I want to replace the bad feelings I have with the good feelings I get from drinking alcohol.

B. (Beliefs): I *must* feel better. I *need* a drink.

C. (Consequences): Drinking.

As you can see from the ABC model presented above, it's not your urge (point A) to replace your bad feelings with good feelings that causes you to drink. It's the beliefs (at point B) that lead to your undesirable consequences (point C).

Imagine how this might look if you held different beliefs at point B:

A. (Activating event): I want to replace my bad feelings with the good feelings I get from drinking.

B. (rational Beliefs): I would *like* another drink and would *like* to feel better, but I *don't need* to feel better and I certainly *don't need* alcohol.

C. (Consequences): Drink sparkling water, not wine.

By using the ABC model to change your beliefs, you change the outcome! When you convince yourself you don't *need* another drink, you more easily keep your urges and drinking in check.

When it comes to changing your drinking habits and reaching your long-term goals, the ABC model is your best friend.

11. HOW TO CONTROL YOUR DRINKING IN THREE MINUTES

THE ABC MODEL DEMONSTRATES WITH clarity the role your beliefs play in your response to your urges. It then becomes a powerful tool for change when you expand it to include points **D**, **E**, and **F**.

In this expanded model, **D** stands for Disputing or questioning the irrational Belief; **E** stands for an Effective new way of thinking; and **F** stands for your new Feelings and behaviors.

At point **D**, you challenge the beliefs you identified at point **B** by asking "Why?" or "What's the evidence for my *must*?" For example, "Why *must* I have a drink right now?" At point **E** you answer this question with effective new perspectives, which aids you in achieving your goals. And at point **F** you describe how you feel and how you will respond when you subscribe to the new way of thinking.

Let's look at an example to illustrate how this process might work for you:

A. (Activating event): I want to replace the bad feelings I have with the good feelings I get from imbibing.

B. (irrational Beliefs): I *must* feel better right now. I *need* a drink.

C. (Consequences of the Belief): Drinking.

D. (Disputing or questioning): Why *must* I feel better right now? What's the evidence I *need* a drink?

E. (Effective new thinking): Much as I would *like* to replace my bad feelings with the good feelings I get from alcohol, there's no law that says I *must* replace these feelings. It's not true I *need* a drink. Similarly, just because I *want* to drink, it does not logically follow that I *must* have one or I *need* one. The idea that I *must* feel better and I *need* a drink leads to behavior which is ultimately self-destructive and sabotages my long-term health, relationship, and financial goals. It would be far better for me to convince myself of the alternative idea, that although I would *like* a drink, I definitely *do not need* one. It's preferable for me to find more constructive means to happiness than through excessive alcohol consumption.

F. (new Feeling and behavior): I feel uncomfortable going without a drink but by convincing myself of the new philosophy I am successful at abstaining.

By regularly writing this expanded ABCDEF model – once or more, every day – you'll conquer your old drinking habits and replace them with new patterns in line with your long-term goals. Once you've had practice using this exercise, it will only take a few minutes to complete it. That's why we call it the *Three Minute Exercise (TME)*.

Study the Three Minute Exercises you'll find here to help you gain a complete and thorough understanding of how to use it to overcome your drinking problem and reach your long-term financial, relationship, and health goals.

12. DO YOU REALLY NEED A DRINK?

THE REASON YOU DRINK MORE, OR MORE often, than you wish lies in escalating a *desire* for a drink (or another drink) into a *demand*. Instead of merely *wanting* a drink, you convince yourself you absolutely *must* have it – you *need* it.

Have you seen a two-year-old lying on the supermarket floor kicking and screaming, *demanding* his mother buy him some candy – immediately! The child does this because he is convinced that he *must* have the candy, he *needs* it, and life is *not worth living* without it. Well, when you demand that you *must* have a drink, you are, in effect, acting in much the same way, only without the histrionics. You're thinking like a two-year-old.

Here's another way of looking at it.

When you *demand* a drink and give in, you're acting like both a tyrant and his faithful servant. You set yourself up as Master of the Universe whose wish becomes a commandment and then you act as the loyal, fearful servant who does exactly as the master demands.

To restrict the amount of alcohol you consume, rebel against the tyrant within you, and then silence it. When your inner tyrant demands a drink, defy the commandment! Challenge yourself by asking, "Why do I *need* a drink? Why *must* I have a drink? Where is the evidence that I will *die* without a drink?" Remind yourself that you *don't have to* have a drink, you *don't need* a drink, and you can survive perfectly well without one.

Convince yourself you *don't need* to feel better, you *don't need* the good feelings you get from alcohol. Unpleasant feelings are just that — unpleasant feelings. Nobody ever died from unpleasant feelings! You can survive with unpleasant feelings even if you distinctly dislike them. You don't *need* to escape from them. You don't *need* another drink!

To silence your inner tyrant, act like a coach or a drill sergeant, screaming back at the tyrant, forcefully reminding it you don't *need* a drink; he or she can survive without it.

A wishy-washy, wimpy rebuttal to your demand for a drink will not work. The more forcefully you remind yourself that you don't need a drink, the more effectively you'll succeed at combating your demands and overcome them, thereby reaching your long-term health goals.

13. SOBRIETY IS NOT THE END OF THE WORLD

WHEN YOU'VE CONVINCED YOURSELF you've *got to* have a drink – that you *need* a drink – you make yourself vulnerable to another type of twisted thinking: you believe it would be *awful*, *terrible*, the *end of the world*, the *worst* thing that could possibly happen to you, if you don't drink.

Of course when you look at these words now, on the screen in front of you, you realize immediately they don't make any sense – they're untrue. But when you feel desperate for a drink, as you do when you convince yourself you *need* one, you genuinely believe going without a drink would be the end of the world.

And when you tell yourself going without a drink would be the end of the world, it seems imperative for you to imbibe. By indoctrinating yourself with the notion that it would be *awful* to deprive yourself of a drink, you reinforce the belief that you *must* have one – immediately!

When you have the urge to drink, you will resist it if you convince yourself, beyond a shadow of a doubt, it would *not* be the end of the world for you to abstain. The more frequently you meaningfully tell yourself it would not be the end of the world to go without a drink – especially at times when you tell yourself you really do *need* one – the easier it will be for you to resist the urge and reach your long-term health goals.

You can use the Three Minute Exercise to practice convincing yourself it's not the *end of the world*; it's not *awful* or *terrible* to go without a drink.

A. (Activating event): I have a strong urge to drink.

B. (Beliefs): It will be *awful* – practically the *end of the world* – if I don't have a drink right now.

C. (Consequences): Drinking.

D. (Disputing): Why is it *awful* if I don't have a drink right now?

E. (Effective new thinking): I would enjoy a drink right now but it would not be the end of the world if I went without. It's not true it would be *awful* to deprive myself. The fact that I have a craving never causes me to conclude going without would be a fate worse than death. Telling myself it would be *awful* to abstain only encourages me to drink and blocks my long-term health goals. I'll get better results by forcefully reminding myself that going without a drink is not the worst thing that could happen. In fact, it's very positive and will greatly benefit me in the long run.

F. (new Feeling and behavior): I resist the urge to drink.

The Three Minute Exercise is once again a powerful tool that can help you overcome the urge to drink by reinforcing – again, and again, and again – the idea that it is not *awful* or *terrible* to go without a drink and to remain sober.

14. HOW TO COPE WITH BEING SOBER

A S WE HAVE SEEN, WHEN YOU TELL yourself you *need* a drink – rather than strongly *desire* one – you overestimate how bad it would be without one, that life would be *awful*. You also tend to underestimate your ability to cope with the feelings that come with abstinence. You repeat to yourself, "I *can't stand* to feel deprived of a drink – especially now."

If you've convinced yourself going without a drink and feeling deprived will kill you, you're likely to insist you *need* alcohol *now*. And once you're convinced abstaining from alcohol will bring about your untimely demise, to save your own skin you reach for the nearest bottle.

Here we have a cycle of destruction. First, you tell yourself you *need* a drink. Second, you tell yourself you'll *die* without one. And third, you tell yourself because you'll die without one, you *need* a drink! The only way you know how to break this cycle is to reach for a drink.

Reflect on it carefully. You'll see whenever you think you *can't stand* something you are, in effect, telling yourself the thing you "*can't stand*" will destroy you in some way. If you *can't stand* a feeling of deprivation, what does this mean? Surely it means the uncomfortable feeling – in this case, the feeling of deprivation – will be the end of you. But how can that be? How can you tell yourself you *can't stand* depriving yourself of a drink at the exact time you are depriving yourself? Obviously, you can stand it. In other words, saying "I *can't stand* discomfort" is a fiction!

Yet there is an alternative, a less destructive way, a way that will preserve your long-term health goals: the Three Minute Exercise!

Michael R. Edelstein

A. (Activating event): I want to replace the bad feelings I have with the good feelings I get from drinking alcohol.

B. (Beliefs): I can't stand depriving myself of the good feelings I get from alcohol.

C. (Consequences): Drinking.

D. (Disputing): Why can't I stand depriving myself of the good feelings I get from alcohol?

E. (Effective new thinking): It's difficult for me to resist the urge to have a drink but it will not kill me to go without. It's also true the feelings I have at the moment are unpleasant, yet it makes no sense to say I can't stand them or that they will destroy me. Telling myself I *can't stand* to abstain from drinking alcohol only encourages me to drink, which is in direct opposition to what I want for myself. I will make healthier choices if I remind myself in this moment I *can stand* what I don't like, going without a drink and remaining sober.

F. (new Feeling and behavior): I experience urges, cravings, and discomfort yet I do not drink.

You can use the Three Minute Exercise to disabuse yourself of the ridiculous and highly destructive idea that you *can't stand* to remain sober.

15. HOW SELF-ABUSE LEADS TO ALCOHOL ABUSE

WHEN PEOPLE STRUGGLE TO CHANGE a behavior unsuccessfully, e.g., compulsive drinking or eating, they have a tendency to put themselves down. They feel ashamed of their failure and, worse, ashamed of themselves.

Perhaps you do this. You may have attempted and failed to change your drinking habits for some time. And now, because you've failed, you give yourself a hard time, calling yourself nasty names – names that devalue you as a human being.

Other people berate themselves mercilessly. They think they can whip themselves into shape through self-denigration. Do you make this mistake? And yes, it is a huge mistake.

According to this line of thinking, if you beat yourself enough and feel thoroughly ashamed of yourself, you'll change your behavior and ultimately be a reformed criminal.

Unfortunately, this tactic seldom works. In reality the reverse is true. The more frequently and viciously you put yourself down, the more likely you are to continue drinking. You drink to bury the bad feelings you have about yourself and to forget what a "rotten person" you are, and what a "failure" you are.

Very often this tactic fails because as a rotten person and a failure you see yourself as undeserving of success. You therefore drink to live up to your image or sabotage your "undeserved" success and further punish yourself for your "rottenness."

You develop a low opinion of yourself by thinking you *should* be able to change, and because you've failed, as you absolutely *must* not, you're an inferior, *worthless* human being. With these vicious words ringing in your ears, your self-esteem plummets.

With these self-recriminations, it's no wonder you feel so bad about yourself. And because you feel bad about yourself, you resort to drinking to feel better.

Self-denigration therefore leads to shame; and – worse – it leads to more drinking. When you put yourself down and verbally attack yourself, rather than helping you to stop drinking, you make it easier for you to continue drinking.

It's bad enough when friends, family, and co-workers put you down for your drinking. But it's far worse and far more destructive when you do it to yourself.

16. WILL SOBRIETY MAKE YOU A BETTER PERSON?

WHEN YOU FEEL SHAME OR SELF-LOATHING after drinking, you do so because you denigrate and devalue yourself as a total human being. In effect, you tell yourself you're worth less than other people; you may even go as far as to consider yourself totally worthless.

If you stop and think about it for awhile you'll soon see rating your value, your self, your humanness, makes no sense. It's impossible to measure human worth and to compare it between two individuals. You can't meaningfully say one person is intrinsically worth more than another. Similarly, you can't increase or decrease your own worth as a human being by abstaining or drinking.

No data or evidence proves there's such a thing as human worth; it's a meaningless concept. Rather there is evidence your actions have worth in terms of achieving (or interfering with) your goals. But if you insist there *is* such a thing as *human* worth, there's no getting away from the fact that it's a definitional concept. You can decide, "I choose to think of myself as having worth merely because I choose it, not because it's an empirical truth."

In summary, although it's a common belief that some people are better – worth more – than others, it makes no sense and is extremely pernicious. It leads to addictions, homicide, and war.

Rating an entire person because of one or two traits and behaviors is an overgeneralization. It equates the evaluation of some of a person's acts with the evaluation of their total personhood. Yet it's illogical to rate a person's value based solely on how well they refrain from drinking or on any of their other behaviors. Because people do so many things, good, bad, and neutral, throughout a day and throughout their lifetime, it's wrong-headed to judge their entire worth based on some of these behaviors.

Each of us consists of so many different parts along with innumerable actions. Consequently we're too complex to be given a single rating. We can rate an aspect of you (for example, your level of sobriety) but we can't rate your total self or your being. Your drinking habits are only one aspect of your entire self – there is far more to you than how much, or how little, you've imbibed today.

Moreover, humans are an ever-changing process. You may have excessively drank yesterday and abstained today. It's illogical to conclude you were worthless yesterday and worthwhile today. In fact, you were an imperfect person who acted poorly yesterday and the same imperfect person who acted well today.

Your ability to perform complex tasks may deteriorate the more you drink. But your worth, your value, does not go up and down depending on your level of sobriety, as though with every drink that passes your lips, your value as a person goes down.

You can, quite legitimately, rate your behavior; you can decide drinking is not a good behavior. This doesn't mean you're not a good person when you drink. Neither does it mean you're a good person when you refrain from drinking. You are not your behavior. What you *do* is not who you *are*. While your actions (as they relate to drinking alcohol) may be foolish, you're not a foolish person – you're merely a person who has acted foolishly on this particular occasion.

Rather than rating yourself and trying to measure your value based on how much or how little you drink, learn to think of yourself as a fallible human being who, like everyone else on the planet, has some good points and some bad points. Instead of putting yourself down for drinking, remind yourself drinking is a choice you make; it is never a determinant of your worth.

17. HOW TO STOP BEATING YOURSELF UP

PERHAPS YOU ARE ONE OF THE MANY people who drink and then beat yourself up for it. Yet there is a better way. Instead of using alcohol to overcome these feelings, you can avoid creating them in the first place with the Three Minute Exercise.

A. (Activating event): I had a night of binge drinking.

B. (Beliefs): I shouldn't have drunk so much. I'm worthless.

C. (Consequences): I feel worthless and ashamed, and drink again to drown my bad feelings.

D. (Disputing): Why shouldn't I have drunk so much? Where's the evidence that I'm worthless?

E. (Effective new thinking): I have made a decision to cut down on my drinking. However, it's not compulsory for me to drink less, it's a choice. There's no reason why I absolutely *must* stop drinking or drink less. Acting against my own best wishes can't magically make me worthless. While my actions are unwise and foolish, my worth as a human being never varies – it doesn't go up and down based on how much or how little I drink. My choice to cut down on drinking does not mean I *absolutely must* stop drinking or cut down on it, although I *passionately desire* to do so. Nor does it logically follow that because I drank more than I had initially intended I become a failure as a person. Putting myself down for drinking only makes me feel bad about myself which often leads me to drink even more alcohol. Therefore telling myself I'm worthless doesn't help me reach my long-term goals – instead, it makes it harder for me to reach them. Rather than telling myself I shouldn't have drunk so much and I'm worthless because I did, I had better convince myself drinking is a choice and I'm determined to succeed at drinking less, no matter how many setbacks I have along the way. It would be better for me to decide and re-decide to abstain rather than give up. And instead of convincing myself I'm worthless for having imbibed more than intended, it would be more useful for me to accept the fact that I'm a fallible human being who will sometimes act against my own best interests. Such actions do not make me worthless. Success involves learning from my mistakes and often going one step back with every two steps forward.

F. (new Feeling and behavior): I feel quite disappointed I overindulged but not worthless and self-loathing. Stick to my original decision to cut down on my drinking.

Get into the habit of using the Three Minute Exercise to overcome any feelings of shame or self-loathing you have after drinking. Even more important, practice writing out the Three Minute Exercises daily getting you prepared for tempting situations that arise unexpectedly. Using this model consistently will make it much easier for you to avoid the temptation of drinking as your means of drowning your bad feelings.

18. WHAT'S LOVE GOT TO DO WITH IT?

HUMAN BEINGS ARE SOCIAL ANIMALS. We usually enjoy the company of others. We frequently prefer to be with friends and family, and we often especially find fulfillment with someone in an intimate relationship.

But we frequently turn our desire for company and affection into a *dire necessity*. We foolishly convince ourselves we *must* have love, respect, and friendship. Creating an irrational *demand* for love and companionship can contribute to your drinking problem, especially when you think you've failed to get the love and companionship you think you *need*.

Here are just some of the ways the *"need"* for love, approval, and friendship can lead to excessive drinking:

1. Because you fear losing the respect and acceptance of others, you make yourself anxious when you try something new and cannot guarantee your success. You're afraid if you fail or look foolish in your attempt, others will think less of you. And because you *can't stand* — at least in your own mind — the prospect of having others think less of you, you avoid taking on new challenges without first being shored up with alcohol.

2. On the other hand, you may take significant risks, doing dangerous or foolish things simply to impress others. You boost your courage to carry out these foolhardy acts by plying yourself with copious quantities of alcohol.

3. You mistakenly make yourself supersensitive to criticism. You feel hurt or angry when others fail to show you the respect you *"must"* have. To help you escape your

bad feelings, you reach for the bottle and set out on another binge.

4. Because you tell yourself you so desperately *need* and *must* have the love and companionship of others, you go out of your way to please them; you do things you normally wouldn't do, merely to impress them. While give and take in relationships is normal and functional, you go overboard with the giving and are unassertive in asking for what you would like. As a result, you become self-loathing and drink to make yourself feel better.

5. If there is no one special in your life at the moment and you're without a partner, you may make yourself depressed and lonely by persuading yourself you absolutely *must* have a lover. Instead of going out and meeting someone, you stay at home and cry into your six-pack of beer.

Escalating a *natural* and *healthy desire* for love and friendship into a *desperate need* can add to your drinking problem and magnify it. Acceptance and companionship are highly desirable for most individuals and it's terrific to pursue them when you can. However, you sabotage your quest for love and friendship if you get convinced you absolutely *must* have it and *can't bear* to be without it. Not only will you almost always sabotage your quest for love and friendship, but you'll also interfere with your long-term health goals by using alcohol to cover up any deficiencies in your love and social life.

When you don't get the love, friendship, or respect you're convinced you *need*, you tend to feel lonely, hurt, anxious, angry, or depressed. And as we've seen throughout this book, you use alcohol to overcome these unpleasant, unhelpful feelings. So your drinking is encouraged by not only your desperation to expunge bad feelings, but also by your "*need*" for love, friendship, and respect.

Whenever you suspect others are looking down on you, don't love you, or don't respect you, you also believe their disapproval is *awful* and you *can't stand* it. You also erroneously use the disapproval of others as a measurement of your worth, and view their disapproval of you as proof of your worthlessness. All of these thoughts and beliefs contribute to your drinking because you use alcohol to dull your emotional pain.

Rather than using alcohol, use rational thinking and the Three Minute Exercise to surrender your need for love.

Susie is a 32-year-old attorney. Although she's successful in her career, her love life is practically non-existent. She has had numerous short-term relationships but none that has lasted longer than six months. She feels depressed and lonely, and drinks heavily every night to drown her sorrows. She knows that drinking only exacerbates the problem and has tried, unsuccessfully, to quit several times. Here's how Susie could use the Three Minute Exercise:

A. (Activating event): I don't have a long-term relationship.

B. (Beliefs): I *must* find someone who will love me. I *need* someone permanent in my life.

C. (Consequences): I feel depressed and lonely, and I drink heavily every night to cope with my loneliness.

D. (Disputing): Why *must* I find someone who will love me? Where's the evidence I *need* someone permanent in my life?

E. (Effective new thinking): I don't enjoy living on my own and would very much *like* to have a loving partner to live with. But there's no data to prove I *have* to have such a partner; it's neither necessary nor compulsory for me to have a live-in lover. Therefore it's not true I *must* find someone who will love me and it's false to suggest I *need* someone permanent in my life. The fact that a long-term relationship is highly desirable for me doesn't logically lead to the conclusion it's absolutely essential. Telling myself I *must* have a lover when, indeed, I don't have one only leads to feeling bad about my total self and my entire life, and contributes to my excessive drinking. It would make more sense to recognize that although love is *desirable*, it's *not necessary* for my happiness; I can be happy without it, although I may be happier with it.

F. (new Feeling and behavior): I'm sad I don't have a long-term, live-in lover but I'm not depressed about it. Instead of drinking every night, I'll join a singles group, take some classes, and pursue on-line dating.

By uprooting her *need* for love, Susie is able to bring her drinking under control and pursue her goals in a far more reasonable and effective manner. Like Susie, you can practice writing the Three Minute Exercise each and every day to overcome your *need* for love, if it's contributing to your drinking problem.

19. PERFECTIONISM, BOOZE AND YOU

HAVING A TALENT AND COMPETENCE in a variety of tasks often makes life easier; you may get things done efficiently the first time rather than redo them over and over. Doing things well can help you in your career as well as in your home life and leisure activities.

Preferring to do things well makes sense. But many people — perhaps you — go beyond only *wanting* to do things well: they *insist* on it. They *demand* perfection in many of their endeavors. And if they can't do something perfectly, they may not even bother trying in the first place.

If you're a perfectionist, you may find it contributes to your drinking problem whenever you fail to meet your perfectionistic standards. Here are some ways your perfectionism may lead to excessive drinking:

1. You feel more than appropriate disappointment and dissatisfaction in all your endeavors when they are less than perfect. Not only are you disappointed with the results, but you *condemn yourself* and you drink to mask your self-loathing.

2. The more perfectionistic your goals, the more likely you are to fail. Your *demand* for perfection makes you anxious, making it harder for you to succeed. And when you inevitably fail to achieve perfection, you reach for the bottle to compensate for your failure.

3. You get behind in your work because you're forever perfecting it. You wouldn't dream of settling for average work, so you go over it interminably, polishing it up as you go. Now that you're behind in your work, you feel

stressed thinking your boss will soon fire you. You then drink to relieve the stress.

4. Perhaps you're outstanding at your job after having spent years developing your skills there. Yet you're bored and desire a new challenge. Being aware you won't immediately succeed at your new job as well as you do your current one, you stay where you are, hating every day of it. So you go home and drink to forget about the deadly, boring job.

5. Your family, friends, and co-workers become irritated with you because of your *demand* for perfection in all you do. Where they settle for second best, you *demand* and *insist* you *must* get everything absolutely, perfectly right. As a result, your relationships are stressed and you drink to dull the stress.

Your perfectionism creates problems for you in a variety of roles — at home, at work, at play, and in your relationships. And when these problems arise, you feel bad and drink to overcome the bad feelings.

Perfectionism is usually based on three fears: (1) the fear you'll perform poorly (2) the fear you'll be seen as inadequate, and (3) the fear of discomfort. Each of these fears stems from a *demanding* attitude; they come from the belief you *absolutely must*, at all times, avoid performing poorly, avoid being seen as inadequate, and avoid discomfort.

When your perfectionism is based on the fear you'll perform poorly, you convince yourself you *must* – you *have to* – live up to a high standard to justify your existence and view yourself as a worthwhile person. You believe you *must not* make mistakes or do substandard work. Rather than merely aiming for a high standard, you insist on an ideal one and *demand* it of yourself.

When your perfectionism is based on the fear you'll be seen as inadequate, you tell yourself that you *must* be viewed as diligent and successful, and it would be *awful* for you to be seen as inadequate.

When your perfectionism is based on the fear of discomfort, you tell yourself that every problem *must* have a perfect solution and you can't rest until you find it. You work tirelessly to keep everything under your control to avoid what you perceive as a disaster if things go wrong. And of course, you convince yourself that you *couldn't stand* to live with the emotional discomfort that would follow if you don't reach the high standards you *demand* of yourself.

Whether your perfectionism is based on the fear you'll perform poorly, the fear of being exposed as inadequate, or the fear of discomfort, you use alcohol whenever your perfect standards are threatened or whenever they lead to emotional discomfort.

Again, the Three Minute Exercise is a healthy substitute for alcohol.

Thomas is a 48-year-old high school English teacher. He puts in long hours of his personal time attempting to perfect his lesson plans. He reads his students' essays several times before writing lengthy comments on each of them. Thomas believes he *must* do his job perfectly well or else he is a substandard teacher, and therefore a substandard human being. The high standards he demands of himself leave him feeling stressed and anxious; he drinks heavily to overcome these unpleasant feelings. Here's how Thomas can replace alcohol consumption with the Three Minute Exercise:

A. (Activating event): I work excessively long hours to ensure I create perfect lesson plans.

B. (Beliefs): I *must* do perfect work at all times.

C. (Consequences): I feel stressed and anxious, and I drink excessively.

D. (Disputing): Why *must* I do perfect work at all times?

E. (Effective new thinking): There is probably no such thing as perfect work. No matter how well I do something, there will always be room for improvement. Although there is merit in striving for excellence, *demanding* perfection is a fool's errand. There's no reason why I *must* do perfect work any of the time, let alone all of the time. The fact that I'd *like* to do my job well and have high regard from my peers does not mean that I *must* do it perfectly well. *Insisting* on perfection — an unattainable goal — leaves me feeling stressed and anxious, and makes it harder for me to quit drinking. I would get much better results for myself, my students, and my long-term health if I convinced myself it's okay to aim for excellence most of the time but I don't *need* to do anything perfectly.

F. (new Feeling and behavior): I take care to ensure my lesson plans and my comments on the students' work are of a high standard but I don't regard it as an absolute *necessity*. As a result, I no longer feel stressed and anxious and I don't have to resort to alcohol to deal with my bad feelings.

Like Thomas, you can use the Three Minute Exercise to overcome your perfectionism and feel relaxed without resorting to booze.

20. DO OTHER PEOPLE DRIVE YOU TO DRINK?

OUR BEHAVIOR IS DRIVEN BY OUR VALUES. We try to do what we believe will advance our values and try to avoid doing what we see as sabotaging them. Unfortunately as fallible human beings we don't always live up to our values and sometimes fail to do what's best.

It's the same with other people. They, like you, attempt to live by their own ideas of right and wrong. And again, like you, they sometimes succeed in living by their values and, as imperfect beings, they sometimes fail.

The values of others – their notions about what's good or bad for them – are often not the same as yours. Frequently they'll act in ways you regard as immoral, stupid, ignorant, or crazy while they see these same behaviors as right, smart, or reasonable.

When other people act in ways you regard as immoral, especially when they treat you unfairly or inconsiderately, it's normal and natural to feel annoyed, frustrated, and disappointed about their actions.

When others treat you poorly, recognize their actions are based on their own human fallibility. If you have the opportunity and it seems appropriate, point out to them how they have impacted you or others and collaboratively discuss other mutually agreeable ways for them to act in future.

But again, human fallibility often gets in the way of effective responses. Instead of accepting others despite their misbehavior and misdeeds, you *demand* – either out loud or silently in your own head – that they *must* act according to your dictates. And when they don't, you feel hurt, angry, stressed, or depressed.

When others treat you unkindly or unfairly, and you experience these unhelpful negative emotions, you reach for the only cure you know: alcohol. Once again, you use alcohol to escape your bad feelings.

When you use alcohol to escape bad feelings after someone has acted unfairly or unkindly toward you, you may irrationally blame them for your actions and your drinking. But your blame is misplaced.

Other people, no matter what they do, do not make you drink. You drink because (1) you disturb yourself by telling yourself unreasonable statements about their behavior, and (2) you self-medicate with alcohol to overcome the disturbed feelings you've created by telling yourself nonsense.

The good news is other people have no control over how much you drink. The frequency with which you drink and the amount you drink, are all within your control. You are the one who has decided to drink after others have treated you badly, and you're the one who can decide not to drink when they treat you badly. You're in the driver's seat.

When other people take advantage of you or treat you poorly, when they act in ways you believe are wrong, you make yourself feel hurt, angry, stressed, or depressed by reinforcing ideas that are patently untrue. In particular, you tell yourself they *shouldn't* behave the way they do and their behavior is *terrible* and *unbearable*.

Edward is smart, business-savvy, and has a good sense of humor. He's the 52-year-old financial manager of a large transport company and often works long hours. However, he has always been a heavy drinker, but recently decided he wanted to stop drinking because it was affecting his health. The owner of the company refuses to pay overtime for the extra hours, and often gives Edward extra work to take home with him. Edward has tried talking to his boss about his unrealistic expectations, but the boss takes no notice. Edward feels angry and resentful towards his boss and, despite his wish to quit drinking, usually drinks several bottles of beer each night to help him forget. You'll notice Edward has three problems: first, his boss takes unfair advantage of him expecting him to do extra work; second, Edward gets angry and resentful – two highly unpleasant, unhelpful emotions; and third, he sabotages his own goal to quit drinking and instead drinks almost every night.

Other than leaving his job and finding another, there's little Edward can do about the first problem. However, his unhelpful feelings and goal-sabotaging actions are within Edward's control. Rather than making himself angry and resentful and resorting to alcohol, Edward can change the way he feels and reduce or eliminate his drinking by using the Three Minute Exercise:

A. (Activating event): My boss takes advantage of me by giving me too much work and refusing to pay me for extra work.

B. (Beliefs): He *must* either give me less work or more money.

C. (Consequences): I feel angry and I drink too much beer every night.

D. (Disputing): Why *must* he either give me less work or more money?

E. (Effective new thinking): There's no law of the universe that says bosses *must* treat their employees fairly. If such a law existed, there would be no unfair treatment of workers anywhere in the world. Since there is unfair treatment of workers throughout the world, it's safe to assume no such law exists. Therefore it's false to assert my boss *must* give me more money or less work. Although I would strongly *prefer* him to give me less work or more money, it doesn't follow from my preference that he *must* give me what I want. Telling myself, *ad nauseum*, he *should* give me less work or more money only makes me feel angry and resentful, feelings I try to escape by drinking despite my goal of quitting. It would be far better for me to accept – without necessarily liking – that my boss will probably continue to treat me unfairly and take advantage of me. I had better get used to the idea that although I *don't like* being taken advantage of, there's no obligation stating my boss *must* give me less work or more money.

F. (new Feeling and behavior): Instead of feeling angry and resentful, I feel annoyed with my boss, and by reminding myself he doesn't *have* to give me what I want, I feel determined to abstain.

If you find yourself feeling hurt, angry, stressed, or depressed about the way others treat you, and you use alcohol to escape from these feelings, regularly practice the Three Minute Exercise instead of resorting to alcohol to help yourself feel better and reach your long-term health and financial goals.

21. HOW TO THINK YOUR WAY TO SOBRIETY

A S WE'VE SEEN, THE KEY TO BRINGING your drinking under control consists of changing the way you think – adopting an entirely new philosophy of life, one without *demands*, *absolutes*, *musts*, *shoulds* or *got to's*. The primary method for accomplishing this involves the Three Minute Exercise. It's not the only tool you can use to change the way you think. Here are other ways you can view alcohol differently:

1. Write down a rational statement you can refer to regularly whenever you're tempted to drink. For example, "Much as I crave a drink, I never *need* one," or "It won't kill me to resist temptation – I can do it." Even better, make this your mantra. Memorize the thought and repeat it to yourself throughout the day. To help you remember, when you arise in the morning, write it on a slip of paper and tape it to the back of your cell phone.

2. List the disadvantages for you of drinking. Review the list at least three times a day until you convince yourself you don't *need* a drink and you can live without one. Then continue to go over it daily to avoid a relapse. Be careful of the temptation to discontinue this practice once you've met your consumption goals. This is when many people fall off the wagon!

3. Read each item on the list vividly, i.e., dwell on each for 30-60 seconds, deeply feeling, experiencing, imagining, and picturing the disadvantage. If your visualization ability is weak, vocalize aspects of the item to make it real. For example if the disadvantage you're focusing on is "risking another DUI," say out loud, "I've lost my license. I'm stuck walking everywhere or waiting impatiently for the bus. I can't visit Brooke anymore. Travelling to the

movies and shopping is now onerous and time-consuming, etc."

4. You can also make a list of the advantages and disadvantages of believing you *need* a drink to cope with difficult situations. Similarly, review this list often and convince yourself you never *must* have a drink.

5. Remind yourself unpleasant feelings are not the end of the world. The more you practice enduring discomfort without resorting to a drink, the better you'll become at resisting temptation.

6. Get into the habit of thinking rationally about alcohol. To help yourself in this regard, read books by Albert Ellis, including *When AA Doesn't Work for You* and *A Guide to Rational Living*. In addition, read *Three Minute Therapy* by Michael Edelstein and *A Guide to Shameless Happiness* by Will Ross.

7. Make recordings of your rational coping statements such as, "I don't *need* a drink," and "I *can stand* being sober." Play these recordings to yourself regularly.

8. Teach REBT philosophy and practice to your friends and family. This helps you become more aware of them, reinforces them, helps you understand them more profoundly, highlights areas of the approach requiring more thought, and aids you in making them an integral part of your belief system.

9. Follow the example of others who have quit drinking. How do they respond under difficult situations and stop themselves from backsliding? Modeling yourself on those who have succeeded, facilitates quitting.

10. Work on developing an unconditional acceptance of reality. Here's how:

· Acknowledge you prefer things to go well for you.

· Recognize situations and events will sometimes go well but often will not.

· Admit that with effort you can sometimes influence the way things are, but oftentimes you can't change events.

· See that you control your emotional and behavioral responses to events by changing your thinking.

· Recognize when things are not to your liking it's not the end of the universe.

· Know that most situations – including the ones you find yourself in at work, at home, and in relationships – are probably not fatal.

· Develop the deep conviction there's no reason why things *absolutely must* be the way you want them to be.

· Be aware that given human fallibility you and others will make mistakes regularly, sometimes large mistakes.

· Convince yourself your failures, mistakes, and limitations *never* magically turn you into an inferior human being.

· Get determined that no matter what happens you'll passionately pursue a fulfilling, joyful, and ethical life.

Continual repetition, reinforcement, and review serve as the best method for adopting new ideas. These thinking exercises offer a variety of ways to inculcate rational, effective beliefs. A new, more functional mode of viewing temptation will result in you being in control of your drinking.

22. HOW TO CHANGE THE WAY YOU FEEL ABOUT ALCOHOL

THE PRIMARY REASON PEOPLE DRINK involves manufacturing good feelings or escaping from uncomfortable ones. Escaping discomfort with drink frequently creates problems; there are more effective ways to feel better, particularly by changing your thinking. But you can also change your feelings directly.

Here are some exercises you can use to work directly with your feelings:

1. Take the rational coping statements you created earlier and repeat them strongly, vigorously, and passionately. For example, "There's absolutely *never* any reason I *must* drink. Never! Never! Never!" Or "Life's tough, too damn bad! I *definitely* can cope without booze!" "No excuses and no debates, I'm *never* going to touch alcohol again, come hell or high water!"

2. You can use your imagination to reduce your reliance on alcohol by employing a three-step technique known as Rational Emotive Imagery. Here's how it works:

STEP 1: Vividly imagine and picture the following: You're in a tempting situation and craving a drink. You're experiencing the powerful urge to drink, but you resist.

STEP 2: As you vividly imagine this, allow yourself to strongly feel in your gut stressed, depressed, or agitated about depriving yourself of a drink. Do Step 2 for just a few seconds.

STEP 3: Still picturing the scene from Step 1, make yourself feel concerned, disappointed, or appropriately frustrated – instead of stressed, depressed, or agitated. How? Since you create your own feelings, with persistence you can modify them. Do this by changing your thoughts. Tell yourself you *can stand* frustration even though you don't like it; convince yourself no law of the universe says you *must* have a drink merely because you strongly *desire* one; remind yourself discomfort and deprivation are just very uncomfortable, never *fatal*, *awful*, *terrible*, or *horrible*.

Practice Rational Emotive Imagery for three minutes twice daily until you've achieved your drinking goals for one month. Then continue the REI once daily or on alternate days to maintain your gains.

3. People sometimes drink to overcome their feelings of shame or embarrassment around others, so they mask their shame with alcohol. Use shame-attacking exercises to overcome your shame in appearing foolish by deliberately acting foolishly in front of others and seeing nothing awful or catastrophic actually happens. For example, at a party deliberately sing loudly and off-key and dance with a poor sense of rhythm; on a bus as each stop approaches, stand up and call out the stop; in a department store loudly announce the time; tell a stranger you were just released from a mental hospital and you're wondering what year it is. Before, during, and after these

exercises forcefully tell yourself you don't turn into a shameful human even if others mistakenly believe you do and you *can bear* feeling uncomfortable while doing the shame-attacks, even though you dislike these feelings.

These feeling exercises will reinforce the rational effective beliefs that help you control your drinking.

23. ACTIONS SPEAK LOUDER THAN WORDS

PERHAPS THE MOST EFFECTIVE WAY OF reinforcing your more functional perspective is by acting on it. You can use a number of REBT behavioral exercises to overcome your addictive thinking. Here are some for you to try:

1. Just do it! Go cold turkey and stop drinking. No matter what happens or how rotten you feel, resist the urge to drink. Period.

2. Deliberately put yourself in situations where you're tempted to drink. Once you're in the situation, refuse to give in to the temptation. *Prove* to yourself you can resist temptation.

3. Reward yourself for staying sober. Set yourself a goal, say, to avoid alcohol for one month. When you reach the goal, buy yourself (non-alcoholic) treats with the money you would have spent on imbibing.

4. From time to time, have a drink. Just one! Show yourself you can drink in moderation without drinking excessively.

5. Develop your social skills. Learn to use assertiveness to get more of what you want in life - at home, at work, and socially. The more often you go after what you want the less disappointed you're likely to be with life and the fewer excuses you'll have to drink.

6. Devote as much time as you can to leisure activities that don't involve alcohol. Make the most of your life. As far as we know, you only have one life so you might as well enjoy it!

7. By taking action and becoming a nondrinker you'll soon see you don't *need* a drink to deal with difficult situations. You'll also discover you can immensely enjoy life without a drink.

8. Overall, avoid daily temptations to drink. Keep alcohol out of your home, don't walk past neighborhood liquor stores or bars, and tell all your friends and family, "For my health and well-being I'm determined never to drink again. Please don't offer me any alcoholic beverages."

24. GETTING ON WITH GETTING SOBER

THE PURPOSE OF THIS BOOK HAS BEEN to teach you powerful concepts and tools for you in achieving your identified life goals. It doesn't tell you what your objective should be. It doesn't insist you either stop or moderate your drinking. It's up to you to choose the most reasonable approach for you to live a better life.

Whether your goal is to reduce the amount of alcohol you drink, the frequency with which you drink, or quit drinking altogether, you now know how to accomplish this. Just as it's up to you to choose your goal, it's up to you how much you'll use those tools to reach your goal. At the same time keep in mind the more frequently and conscientiously you practice what you've learned here, the sooner and more thoroughly you'll succeed. Practice makes near perfect!

You'll be happier and more productive if you're motivated by strong preferences rather than by absolutistic demands. Your likelihood of success will be greatly enhanced if you employ the practical, rational steps we describe, all the while being aware there's no guarantee of *immediate* success. Have patience and take a long-term perspective. Face discomfort now for more comfort in the long-run.

Throughout this book you've seen the many excuses people use to drink excessively; and the many ways to employ the Three Minute Exercise along with a variety of other strategies to beat your addiction.

It's possible your particular rationalizations or circumstances were not mentioned. However, a wonderful feature of the Three Minute Exercise lies in its adaptability to meet your requirements for success.

The Three Minute Exercise puts you in charge of your life, including if and when you drink alcohol. If you do choose to drink, it puts you in control of the amount and frequency. In effect, by practicing the Three Minute Exercise you reduce or eliminate the usefulness of attending self-help groups or therapy. You act as your own therapist!

It's important to recognize all of the exercises we present are designed to be done daily as preparation for tempting situations. Practice these tools religiously and make it second nature to do so.

In addition, progress mixed with lapses often makes up the learning process. You'll ultimately succeed if you refuse to give up in the face of setbacks. Most individuals who overcome their compulsive drinking are not the ones who expect immediate or perfect success, rather it's those who get adamantly determined to persevere no matter how difficult the bumps are along the way.

Work and practice, work and practice: these hold the key to overcoming most of life's difficulties. Problem drinking is no exception.

CONTACT DR. EDELSTEIN

Names and other personal details of the case histories cited have been changed, and in some instances details of two or more different clients have been combined in one composite personality.

Both authors had input on every page of this book and the precise wording was a joint effort. "We" refers to both authors, while "I" always refers to Dr. Edelstein.

This publication is designed to provide accurate and authoritative information in regard to the subject matter covered. It is sold with the understanding that the publisher (Will Ross) did not engage in rendering psychological, medical, or other professional services. If you require expert assistance or counseling, please contact the lead author:

Dr. Michael R. Edelstein
Phone, Skype, and in-person clinical psychology practice

San Francisco
415-673-2848 (24 hours)
DrEdelstein@ThreeMinuteTherapy.com
www.ThreeMinuteTherapy.com

ABOUT THE AUTHORS

Dr. Michael R. Edelstein is a San Francisco clinical psychologist with an in-person, Skype, and telephone therapy practice. He is a Certified Rational Addictions Therapist and was the San Francisco Professional Advisor for SMART Recovery. He is the author of the best-selling *Three Minute Therapy*, which has chapters on addictions and a variety of emotional problems. He trained with Dr. Albert Ellis and supervises addiction counselors in the REBT/CBT treatment of addictions. For more info go to: http://www.ThreeMinuteTherapy.com.

Will Ross tutored REBT self-helpers and was the author and publisher of online REBT self-help materials. He was the webmaster and co-founder of REBTnetwork.org, established in 2006 to promote Rational Emotive Behavior Therapy (REBT) and the life and work of its creator, Dr. Albert Ellis, Ph.D.

68977865R00062

Made in the USA
San Bernardino, CA
09 February 2018